(

EcoZones

ARCTIC TUNDRA

Lynn M. Stone

ROURKE ENTERPRISES, INC.
Vero Beach, FL 32964

Photo Credits:

© 1989 Rourke Enterprises, Inc.

Library of Congress Cataloging in Publication Data

Stone, Lynn M.
  Arctic Tundra / by Lynn M. Stone.
    p. cm. — (Ecozones)
  Includes index.
  Summary: Examines the arctic tundra as an ecological niche and describes the plant and animal life supported there.
  ISBN 0-86592-436-8
  1. Tundra ecology—Arctic regions—Juvenile literature.
2. Tundra—Arctic regions—Juvenile literature.   [1. Tundra ecology.   2. Ecology.]   I. Title.   II. Series: Stone, Lynn M. Ecozones.
QH541.5.T8S76   1989
574.5'2644—dc20   89-32743
                                                                            CIP
                                                                             AC

Contents

ARCTIC TUNDRA

The great north woods girdles much of central Canada and the northern United States. Much of it is wilderness, a broad, green belt of evergreen trees speckled with lakes and bogs. Moose dabble in the wetlands. Lynx prowl like shadows in the dark forest, and beavers dam cold streams. This is rugged country, but north of the evergreens lies the Arctic tundra. A vast expanse of land that creeps north to the Arctic Ocean, the tundra is even more harsh and forbidding.

The tundra is a nearly treeless mat of grasses, sedges, mosses, lichens, flowers, and shrubs. It is the northern home of wolves, caribou, musk-oxen, and, in summer, clouds of water birds. The tundra sprawls northward from the **tree line**, the northernmost latitude at which trees can grow. It is bounded by the Arctic Ocean and the Bering Sea on the north. On the North American mainland, it extends westward from the coast of Labrador, Canada, to the northeastern shores of Hudson Bay, a giant thumb of the Arctic Ocean. From the west coast of Hudson Bay, the tundra

Opposite *Musk ox, shedding its winter coat, grazes on sparse plants of Ellesmere Island, Canada.*

fringes northern Canada and the north and west coasts of Alaska.

Tundra does not follow precise lines. It dips here and there into the woodlands. Occasionally, pockets of tundra develop in the evergreen forests of the far north. Wherever the woodland begins to fail on its northern edges, tundra and a sparse cover of trees join in a union of forest-tundra, often called **taiga**.

Along with the North American ground it covers in Alaska and mainland Canada, tundra peppers the multitude of Canada's Arctic islands. Collectively, these islands are called the Canadian **archipelago**. The largest among them is Baffin Island, which lies between the Arctic Ocean and Hudson Bay.

The largest of all the Arctic islands is Greenland, which is several times the size of Baffin. Greenland, however, while part of North America, is neither Canadian nor American; it is closely affiliated with Denmark. Much of Greenland is permanently frozen in **glaciers**, gigantic rivers of ice. The ice supports no vegetation, but Greenland has tundra on its ice-free ground.

Arctic tundra has a **circumpolar** distribution. That means it circles the

TUNDRA

northern tip of the globe. Beyond the limits of North America, tundra covers numerous Arctic islands and fringes the entire northern boundary of the Soviet Union. Worldwide, tundra occupies roughly three million square miles, about one-twentieth of the earth's surface. Most North American tundra lies above 60° north latitude. In northeast Canada and western Alaska, tundra reaches south to 54° north latitude.

The word *tundra* originated in Finland. The English language borrowed the word from the Russian *toondra,* which referred to a marsh grassland with frozen soil underneath. That is a fair description of tundra, for the tundra is sometimes called the "Arctic prairie," a reference to North America's treeless grasslands far to the south. However, unlike the true prairie of mid-continent, the tundra in underpinned by permanently frozen ground. Additionally, tundra exists in an entirely different set of conditions than the grasslands of mid-continent. Although its openness begs for comparison to prairie, the tundra **environment** supports a different community of plants and animals than the American prairie.

Most of the tundra across the Northwest Territories in mainland Canada is relatively flat or rolling. In northern Alaska and on several of Canada's Arctic islands, the tundra spreads part way up the slopes of mountain ranges.

From the air, the tundra of the Northwest Territories, called Canada's Barren Grounds, is an endless tapestry of lakes. Many of them appear almost perfectly round. Interspersed among them are **polygons**, circles of stones, and **pingos**, tiny cone-shaped hills contributed to the landscape by frost heaves. **Eskers**, narrow ridges of glacial fill, stand as widely-scattered sentries.

Upon closer inspection, the parts of the tundra that are not under water are a carpet woven and anchored by plants. It is a lumpy carpet, to be sure, split, tattered, and often mushy. It is pocked by numerous shallow pans of water that are so obvious from the air. Farther north, the carpet of tundra becomes threadbare. Patches of ground lie uncovered, and the rocky ground looks more like desert than prairie.

The Arctic tundra of summer and the Arctic tundra of winter are as different as the summer and winter coats of Arctic foxes. In the Far North, winter dominates the year. As early as August, after a brief summer fling, the tundra

Below Tundra is a mat of grasses, sedges, mosses, lichens, wildflowers, and shrubs. Snow goose nest at left.

has cold pangs and the onset of shorter days. Winter arrives with wolf-like suddenness, and for three-quarters of the year the tundra is frozen hard as steel. Temperatures fall to 60°F and 70°F below zero. Although Arctic snowfall is not heavy, the flakes may be driven by fierce, moaning winds. Winter's iron hand lifts in late May. Longer periods of sunlight and increasing temperatures begin to ease away the ice and snow. Patches of last summer's yellow and brown tundra mat appear. Wobbling lines of waterfowl appear overhead. The tundra summer has begun.

Many people associate the words *tundra* and *Arctic* with cold. During the winter, the frozen tundra is, indeed, frigid and hostile. Although no one will mistake the summer tundra for Miami Beach, the tundra is a surprisingly sensitive and even pleasant place in midsummer. Temperatures often exceed 70°F, and there is virtually no darkness; the sun stays above the horizon nearly all day. The warmth and long periods of sunlight create an explosion of plant and animal life.

With the snow disappearing, old tundra plants are uncovered for plant-eating animals, and new plants begin to bloom. The tundra becomes a magnet

for legions of birds that nest upon it. The arrival of hundreds of thousands of birds on the Arctic tundra is one of the great natural spectacles in North America. The birds arrive in broad, wavering V's, in loose strings, and in tightly knit buckshot patterns. Their calls, riding on the wind, identify them: Canada, snow, and white-fronted geese; eiders, old-squaws, and scoter ducks; tundra swans, loons, sandhill cranes, gulls, jaegers, shorebirds, and songbirds. More than 100 species in all, they spiral down toward traditional nesting sites on rocky

Above *Canada geese and dozens of other kinds of water birds migrate to the tundra to nest.*

islets and gravel ridges and in tangles of grass.

Arctic deer, known as Barren Ground caribou, file by the thousands onto the tundra from the sanctuary of northern forests where they spend their winters. They represent the last of the great herd migrations in North America. The buffalo migrations across the American heartland ended over 100 years ago when the herds were shot to pieces.

Incredible swarms of blackflies and mosquitoes descend upon the tundra pasture, too. They make life miserable for the caribou, but they are food for birds.

For a few weeks, the tundra is transformed into a community of urgent, rampant life. The green tundra mat itself is an endless source of food for the tundra **herbivores**, the plant-eaters. In turn, the meat-eaters, the **carnivores**, find a bounty of plant-eating prey on which to feed.

The tundra in summer is not, of course, always basking in warmth and sunshine. Summer days can be balmy and bright, or they can be harsh and bleak. A sudden cold front, running with a rain or snow squall, can doom a nesting season for birds. The short Arctic summer has no slack for second and third attempts at nesting. The scramble of tundra life has to be compacted into a few short weeks between June and September. In late August lines of snow geese begin trailing off to the south, signaling the return to winter. Thousands of sandhill cranes climb sun-bound, their bugled "wharoooo, wharoooo" drifting down onto a browning tundra.

Like a shooting star, the Arctic summer is intense, but it flames out quickly. Winter is never more than a few inches away in the frozen soil below the tundra.

TYPES OF TUNDRA

Thousands of years ago, glaciers covered much more of North America than they do now. When they gradually retreated northward, much of the land that they left exposed grew up in tundra vegetation. The climate and soil could support tundra growth but not trees. Later, the climate warmed. Forests developed where much of the tundra had been. Most of the tundra that remained was in the Far North, the area loosely referred to as the Arctic.

The Arctic region has never been perfectly defined. There is a frozen, continental land mass at the South Pole called Antarctica. There is no Arctic continent, however. Geographers have established an imaginary line at latitude 66° north marking the Arctic Circle. Still, many of the plants, animals, soil conditions, and climate conditions that we associate with Arctic life north of that line also occur well south of that line. Tundra, remember, dips to 54° north latitude.

In any event, the tundra of the North is Arctic tundra. But what about patches of tundra that still lingered in

Opposite *Colorful autumn taiga marks the last stand of trees in the foothills of the Alaska Range, Denali National Park.*

southern Canada and the United States long after the glacial retreat and the rise of forests? Those patches survived isolated on high ground in windswept mountain ranges where the environment remains somewhat like that of the Far North. These **relict** tundra meadows are called alpine tundra. They begin at altitudes where trees can no longer grow. In some places, such as in New England, the tree line climbs only to 4,000 feet above sea level. Elsewhere, alpine tundra develops at 8,000 to 10,000 feet, such as in the Colorado Rockies.

Alpine tundra doesn't harbor the animal life associated with the Arctic tundra, nor are the plant **species** identical. In addition, alpine tundra typically receives more precipitation than Arctic tundra. The mountain soil is rocky, however, and water tends to run off rather than settle in the maze of pools that typifies Arctic tundra. Nevertheless, alpine tundra bears a strong resemblance to the Arctic tundra in the sharing of meadows, rock gardens, lichens, and mosses. Like the Arctic tundra, alpine tundra develops close to the ground. Punishing mountain winds keep plant life cropped low, just as Arctic winds trim the northern tundra.

In the Arctic tundra are several different **habitats**, each a little world within the tundra as a whole. Each habitat represents a somewhat different community of plants and animals. Around wetlands, for example, moisture-loving tundra plants grow. On gravel ridges, where the ground is well-drained, miniature forests of lichens and moss develop. In areas of fairly rich, moist soil, the tundra may have a brushy cover of small willows, birches, and alders. These are tree species, certainly, but as in the other tundra habitats where

Above *Alpine tundra above tree line in Colorado Rockies.*

17

trees persist, they never grow to normal size. Elsewhere, the tundra may be a spongy mat of grass clumps, or **tussocks**.

In the northernmost extremities of the Arctic, tundra plants are sparse. Sand dunes and ribs of exposed gravel protrude. Sheltered hollows, where snow defies sunlight for 10 or 11 months of the year, resist plants' efforts to gain a footing. In other regions the tundra partially covers mountain slopes. As the mountain rises, tundra plants, becoming less and less able to cope with increasing exposure, wind, and loose soil, vanish.

The southern edges of the tundra meet the forest-tundra, or taiga. Taiga is neither true forest nor true tundra. It is a transition zone. Soil and climate conditions here are such that both sides, tundra and forest, give some way to the other.

The taiga is a colorful life zone, especially in autumn when spruces stand green in a leafy quilt of browns, yellows, and reds. The ground cover of taiga is a clinging web of berry-producing shrubs, grasses, mosses, and spongy clumps of caribou lichen. Its spruces, the last sentinels of the **conifer**, or evergreen, forests, often lean crazily, undermined by frost upheavals and thin soil.

As a transition zone, the forest-tundra is attractive to many animals that normally live in forest or tundra. Moose, for instance, and several tree-nesting birds occupy the taiga. The more open, tundra-like sections of taiga are homes to ground-nesting tundra species of birds.

MAKING OF THE TUNDRA

Like other natural communities, the Arctic tundra is a product of several special circumstances. One of the major elements that shapes tundra is **permafrost**.

Permafrost is frozen soil. It occurs wherever freezing exceeds the climate's ability to thaw. Permafrost underlies about 80 percent of Alaska and 50 percent of Canada, including the Canadian and Alaskan tundra. In some parts of Alaska, permafrost reaches down 1,300 feet. Permafrost measures nearly a mile deep in one Siberian site.

Permafrost is a remarkable natural refrigerator. In 1900, a woolly mammoth was discovered in the permafrost of northeastern Siberia. This species of ancient elephant had been extinct for thousands of years when it was found. This particular mammoth had probably been in the frozen ground for 40,000 years. A scientist who examined the beast said that "the flesh . . . which is fibrous and marbled with fat, is dark red in color and looks as fresh as well-frozen beef." The scientist did not sample the meat, but before he arrived, several wolves did.

Opposite *Permafrost created these polygons in the northern tundra of Canada.*

Each spring the upper layer of permafrost, coaxed by warmer temperatures, thaws. It is this thin band of soil, called the active layer, that allows plants to take root and grow during the Arctic summer. Trees, on the other hand, can root only if at least 18 inches of soil thaws. Pine trees need eight feet of loose soil. Birches, white spruce, and balsam—typical trees of the northern forests—need four feet of thawed soil. Black spruces can manage with 18 inches.

In the tundra-covered portions of North America, fewer than 18 inches of soil thaw. Eighteen inches is fine for the hundreds of plant species that grow in the tundra, but it is inadequate for trees of normal stature.

Permafrost is also responsible in another way for the growth of tundra plants. It traps moisture above it, in the few inches of thawed soil. That moisture is critical for the development of most plants. The underlying ice of permafrost simply does not absorb the water that collects on the tundra. A Canadian plant expert observed that without permafrost the tundra would be largely "a lifeless desert."

As it is, tundra has a desert-like precipitation. That seems odd and highly unlikely since the tundra is a checkerboard of ponds and lakes. Yet the majority of the Arctic receives less than 10 inches of precipitation, most of it in summer rain. The Mojave Desert has greater rainfall! On Ellesmere Island in the Canadian Arctic, the average precipitation is less than two inches.

Precipitation and cold conspire to shape the tundra's topography, or rise and fall of its landscape. Much of the tundra is lumpy, cracked, and furrowed. The forces of freezing and thaw are constantly at work, creating tremendous upheavals of ice, rocks, earth, and plants. As moisture in the ground freezes, it expands. The pressures often push upwards, lifting earth in mounds and hills and creating fractures in the ground. Some of the frost action creates curiously uniform formations of rocks and earth.

Another factor in the development of tundra is the polar climate, defined as a climate in which the average temperature of July does not exceed 50 degrees. That type of climate roughly follows the tree line. In addition to the long, cold, dark winters and cool, bright summers of the polar environment, the tundra is raked by stinging, drying winds. Those winds help restrict plant growth to the kind typical of the tundra.

PLANTS
OF THE TUNDRA

Several hundred species of flowering plants grow on the tundra along with non-flowering plants—mosses, lichens, algae, and fungi. Considering the harsh polar climate and thin soil in which most of these plants develop, they are indeed hardy organisms.

Arctic plants have evolved by being able to cope with their rigorous environment. They have developed special features, or **adaptations**, that allow them to live in a situation where most other plants could not.

One adaptation to life in the Arctic is chemical antifreeze. Scientists have learned that many Arctic plants do not freeze and die because they produce a chemical that protects them. Another adaptation is a root system that spreads horizontally rather than vertically. Plants would have no future in attempting to send roots downward into permafrost.

A third adaptation of most Arctic plants is the development of specialized leaves that limit **transpiration**. Green plants lose vital moisture through their leaves in a process called transpiration.

Opposite *Lapland rosebay is a miniature rhododendron. Its bright blossoms help attract insects.*

Small, leathery leaves and leaves with waxy or hairy surfaces are typical of tundra plants and helpful in limiting water loss. The interwoven, mat-like spread of tundra plants also helps slow water loss both from the mat and from the ground.

The Arctic tundra does have a scattering of birches and willows, in miniature, of course. To survive, the dwarf trees have shallow, spreading roots. They cling wherever possible to rocks for shelter from the abrasive wind. A century-old birch may stand no taller than fallen caribou antlers.

One of the brightest spots on the summer tundra is the deep-pink blossom of rosebay, a shrub in miniature. The rosebay rhododendron looks nearly identical to the blooms of the rhododendrons that rise 25 feet in the eastern United States.

Buttercups, poppies, saxifrage, and dozens of other flowering plants, best seen from lying on the ground, brighten the tundra. But one of the Arctic's most important plants, lichen, never flowers at all.

Lichens are a product of two plant groups—algae and fungi. Their marriage produces lichen, an extremely hardy plant that can grow where most plants cannot, like the surfaces of rocks. Tundra rocks are painted by lichens in black, white, yellow, and orange. Some are so specialized that they grow only in places enriched by bird droppings.

Lichens peel like old scrolls, develop as crusts, or even stand like brittle toy soldiers. But lichens' attractive appearance belies their real value to the tundra community. Some lichens gradually reduce rock material to soils. Others represent a major source of food for plant-eating animals. The cladonia lichens, commonly called caribou moss, are a favorite of caribou. Cladonia grow in delicate, lacy clusters on both the tundra and in the "drunken forest" of tilting black spruces on the tundra edge.

ANIMALS OF THE TUNDRA

The growth of tundra plants makes the tundra suitable for animals. Relatively few animal species have been able to adapt to tundra living on a year-round basis, but each summer the ranks are swelled by the arrival of migratory birds and the caribou. Animals that have the capability to leave the tundra when winter arrives are not reluctant to take advantage of the food and safety afforded by the summer tundra.

The animal life of the tundra ranges from **invertebrates**, little animals without a backbone, to 700-pound musk-oxen. Tundra invertebrates include insects, mites, spiders, and snails, among others. Some of these creatures feed on plant matter. Others dine on their neighbors.

Opposite *Willow ptarmigan (shown) and rock ptarmigan live throughout the year on tundra.*

Two of the legendary insects of the tundra are mosquitoes and blackflies. Less obvious to man, but of concern to caribou, is the warble fly. A fuzzy relative of the housefly, the warble fly attaches its eggs to the hairs of a caribou's stomach in the fall. Larvae emerge from the eggs and tunnel into the caribou's flesh. They spend the winter in the caribou, emerging as adults in the summer.

Tundra ponds, with their ice bottoms, are usually too shallow for fish, but tundra streams often contain grayling. These are cold, silver-black, trout-sized fish. Slick as river stones, they have broad, fan-like dorsal fins, small mouths, and a big hunger for insects.

Reptiles and amphibians are nearly absent from the tundra world. The Hudson Bay toad and wood frog are exceptions. They just reach some of the lower reaches of tundra.

Most tundra birds are visitors. They **migrate** to the tundra each spring and migrate from the tundra each fall. As far as we know, birds make the long journey to the Arctic because they find food, safety, and isolation from most human disturbance. They also come because their ancestors have been flying here each year for thousands of years. A migratory tradition has been established, just as human adults set aside certain days each year for celebration and teach their children to do the same each year.

Ancestors of the tundra's nesting birds may have been using the tundra 20,000 years ago. Ice covered much of the continent then, but left clear some northern areas.

Tundra-nesting birds arrive from the United States, Asia, and the Caribbean. Golden plovers fly north to the tundra from South America. The long distance champion, however, is the Arctic tern. A fish-eating bird, the Arctic tern winters in the Antarctic, at the other end of the globe.

Birds that nest on the tundra are ready to select their nest sites immediately. Courtship and mating have usually taken place elsewhere on the migration route. Snow geese, for example, arrive at one of their **colonies** in the Northwest Territories around June 1. Within three or four days they have staked out a nest site. The female plucks down from her breast and settles by a

Below *Snow goose on nest anchored by dwarf willows, sheltered by lichen-spotted rock.*

rock or among tiny willows. Within the week, she has a clutch of five or six eggs in her down nest. During the fourth week in June, her eggs and the eggs of almost every other snow goose in the colony hatch.

The hatch corresponds to the bloom of Arctic plants and the emergence of insects, both of which are goose fodder. The goslings grow quickly. Snow geese and their web-footed relatives abandon the tundra in August and September along with the scores of other water birds. The only birds that remain to overwinter are snow buntings, redpolls, ravens, rock ptarmigan, willow ptarmigan, and snowy owls. When prey is scarce, snowy owls travel south, too, sometimes invading the northern United States.

The tundra's bird population, for the most part, lives off the vegetable matter and invertebrates. The exceptions are the **predators**, birds that live on a diet made up at least partly of larger animals. The snowy owl preys chiefly on lemmings. Gulls and their relatives, the jaegers, take eggs and young from other birds. Sandhill cranes are truly **omnivorous**. Normally they eat vegetable matter, but they sometimes spear baby birds. Goshawks, peregrine falcons, and gyrfalcons are meat-eating birds of prey usually found over coastal tundra.

Without the advantages of flight, mammals of the tundra are more or less forced to live off the tundra throughout the year. The migratory caribou of the Barren Grounds avoid that fate by trekking to the sanctuary of spruce forests. Caribou on the northern islands, where there are no trees, take shelter on the lee side of rocks and mountains.

The small plant-eating mammals include two species of lemmings, Arctic ground squirrels, and Arctic hares. Larger herbivores are the caribou and musk-oxen. One herbivore or another provides a source of meat for the furry carnivores—weasels, Arctic foxes, wolves, and the Barren Ground race of grizzly bear. Polar bears rarely venture onto tundra. They are essentially animals of the Arctic ice pack.

One of the most important animals in the Arctic chains of life is the lemming. Plump and mouse-like, lemmings arc extremely **prolific**. During years of lemming abundance, the population of their predators—owls, foxes, and weasels—soars. Sadly, lemmings sometimes over-graze a section of tundra. Having eaten themselves out of home,

Right *The lemming is one of the most important animals in the Arctic food chains.*

Right *Grizzly bears (shown) roam northern tundra. Polar bears prowl Arctic ice pack at sea.*

their numbers fall. Predator numbers correspondingly fall, too, although not before they may make unusually high inroads on bird populations.

Another important Arctic grazer, and one whose population is also **cyclical**—that is, it periodically rises and falls—is the caribou. Both sexes of caribou are antlered, and they are stockier and more block-like than their relatives, the deer that live farther south. They are also uniquely adapted to bone-chilling cold. Their entire bodies are covered by long, hollow hairs under which is a layer of curly underfur. Even caribou muzzles are furred. They have special adaptations for breathing cold air and for circulating blood into their legs. In addition, they can live on a diet of low-protein lichens that would starve other large grazing animals.

Many mysteries surround the migration of caribou. What ignites the onset of migration? How do they find their way across hundreds of miles of wilderness? Whatever its roots, caribou migration is relentless. The herds travel up to 30 miles each day. They cross lakes, ice-littered rivers, and treacherous snow fields.

The spring migration takes the caribou from forest and mountain retreats to traditional calving grounds on the tundra. Seventy-five percent of the herd's calves are born within five days. Within a few days of their arrival, the herds are moving again, looking for new pasture and escape from insects. An adult caribou can lose up to a quart of blood each week to its insect pursuers.

Perhaps 50 percent of caribou calves die during their first month. They can be killed by unusually heavy or crusted snow, drowning, insects, or wolves. The survivors—adults and calves alike—split up into smaller herds with the first August frosts. The insect menace passes, and caribou bulls begin to show their autumn finery—long, heavy antlers, and sleek, silver-brown coats.

The wolf is a major predator of caribou. Wolves settle for lesser animals, even rodents, but the general well-being of a tundra wolf pack is dependent upon its ability to kill caribou. Wolves typically kill very young or old caribou. Their attacks help to maintain a healthy caribou herd as well as a healthy wolf pack.

Being social animals, wolves live and hunt in packs, each of which has its leaders and followers. Packs rarely number more than 20.

Wolves are a mixed bag of colors. They may be brown, buff, gray, black, or some blend of colors. The wolves of the Canadian Arctic islands, often labeled Arctic wolves, are usually white.

The little Arctic fox, like the wolf, is a wild dog. Foxes prosper when the lemming population is high and nesting birds abound. Foxes stash some of their summer kills in rock larders for use in the winter. Sometimes they are forced to

leave the tundra and scavenge the remains of seals killed by polar bears on the pack ice.

Just as tundra plants have evolved adaptations to live in the polar environment, so have tundra animals. The Arctic fox and the chicken-like ptarmigan are magicians at camouflage. When a ptarmigan flattens herself against her clutch of eggs, she is nearly impossible to see. Only her bright eyes may give her whereabouts away; she looks as if she has been woven into the tundra. The Arctic fox has a mottled coat of earth colors in the summer, a good match for

Above *Magnificent bull caribou, sleek and well-groomed for autumn, grazes in shrubby tundra of Alaska.*

its surroundings. Each winter, the fox and the ptarmigan turn white.

The Arctic fox's small, round ears are another adaptation. Small ears lose less body heat than the larger ears of foxes in warmer regions.

Other adaptations for life on the tundra include the heavy coats of several animals, such as the musk-ox. Insects, like some plants, have a chemical resistance to freeze. The caribou has large, soft foot pads in the summer for traction on soggy tundra, and ptarmigan have feathered "snowshoes" for easier movement in winter.

Just because an animal lives on the tundra doesn't mean that it lives everywhere on the tundra. Some areas are much more suitable for certain species than others. Musk-oxen, for example, live only in a very few, far northern localities. Snow geese number in the hundreds of thousands. But the snow goose colonies are all restricted to coastal tundra where there are tidal rivers. Rock ptarmigan live in the high, driest tundra. Willow ptarmigan live on moister, grassier tundra.

THE FLOW OF ENERGY

In whatever tundra habitat it occupies, each of the plants and animals of the Arctic tundra has its **niche**, its place and function in the **ecosystem**. The tundra is a system of natural orderliness, not a haphazard collection of living things. It is an environment in which organisms are useful to each other. Relatively few species of plants and animals occupy niches on the tundra, but for the plants and animals that do play out their lives on the tundra, survival is dependent upon an orderly flow of energy.

Energy provides organisms with the ability to function in their respective niches. An Arctic fox, for example, is both hunter and scavenger. Hunting and scavenging are niches—jobs—which the Arctic fox fills at different times. The fox's ability to hunt is dependent upon its ability to produce the energy to hunt. Energy is gained from food. As long as the fox can hunt successfully, it will be able to eat and produce energy.

The energy that the fox produces is the result of a food chain through which energy passes. It neither begins with the fox nor with the lemming that the fox may gobble up. In the Arctic tundra, food chains are quite simple because the number of life forms is limited. Through typical food chains we can see how energy flows on the tundra.

Plants are the first link in Arctic tundra food chains. Plants are **producers**. They convert sunlight and nutrients from air and soil into food. Thus, they provide food for themselves. When a lemming munches on a leaf or stem, it unlocks the plant's food—and energy— for itself. The energy, in the form of food, has now passed from sun and air and ground to a plant. Through the plant it has passed to a herbivore, in this instance a lemming.

The lemming is a **consumer**; it eats, or consumes, what is produced by a basic producer, the plant. The fox is a consumer, too. But it doesn't consume plants, at least not directly. Rather, it consumes plant eaters, like the lemming. When the fox devours the lemming, energy has flowed in another time and into another link in the chain.

Lemmings breed in abundance. The loss of one—or thousands—will not affect the animal's ability to survive comfortably as a species. When a fox seizes a lemming, energy moves one

Above *Dall sheep graze on tundra plants in high meadows of Alaska and north-western Canada.*

more link. There aren't nearly as many foxes as lemmings, so there is no danger of foxes wiping out the lemming population. Yet if no lemmings at all were killed by foxes, the fox population might be in jeopardy. And without the fox and other predators, the lemmings might overpopulate and permanently damage the tundra mat. Notice the balance here. Tundra plants abound if they aren't overgrazed. They aren't overgrazed if the herbivores don't overwhelm them. If predators are available to check the number of herbivores, the tundra mat

Above *Caribou rack among boulders is silent testament to the flow of energy from herbivore to carnivore on the tundra.*

41

will remain healthy and the entire ecosystem will operate in balance.

In another simple tundra food chain, a caribou eats plants and a wolf eats the caribou. Energy moves two links. Some plants and a caribou would appear to be "losers" in this chain while the wolf, at the top of the chain, "wins." But there are still more plants than caribou and more caribou than wolves. Each species, then, although preyed upon by another, is still successful. Ultimately, the wolf will die. **Decomposers**, little and often microscopic plants and animals, will feed on the wolf's body. The dead wolf becomes their source of energy. Eventually the tissue that was wolf will be broken down by decomposers into compounds that unite with the soil or are returned to the air. These compounds of the former wolf are used by growing plants which may, some day, be eaten by a caribou. And, yes, the caribou may be eaten by a wolf.

CONSERVATION OF THE TUNDRA

For thousands of years the Arctic's isolation protected it from being ruined. Even now, comparatively few people have set foot on the tundra.

The native people of the North, the Aleuts and Inuit (Eskimos), reached North America from eastern Siberia some 6,000 to 10,000 years ago. A land

Below *Tundra lake glimmers in McConnell River Migratory Bird Sanctuary during a midnight sunset in July, Northwest Territories.*

bridge existed at that time between Alaska and Siberia. The natives hunted from kayaks, canoes, and dog sleds. Their populations were modest, and they were nomads, moving from one location to another in their quest for food. Their activities did not injure the living system of the Arctic.

European explorers began visiting the coastal Arctic, however, as early as the late 1500s. They brought tools, weapons of steel, disease, alcohol, and a destructive way of life. Over a long period of time, native traditions eroded in the conflict between old and new ways. The conflict is still going on.

In recent years, the tundra itself has paid some of the consequences of discovery and exploration. Serious questions exist about the tundra's future. Once an unspoiled showplace of plants and animals, the tundra was largely an unpeopled wilderness. Most of that primitive beauty and much of the tundra's wildlife remain, but the Arctic's isolation, its separation from the rest of North America, has ended forever. In 1968, engineers confirmed that a reservoir of oil and natural gas lay buried along Alaska's Arctic coast. The Arctic rush began in earnest. Roads, a pipeline, and attendant service areas were built.

Numerous other projects designed to find oil and minerals or produce electricity are being undertaken in the Arctic. Some of this work is being done very carefully with an eye to the welfare of the ecosystem, but the tundra scars easily. One problem facing Canada and the United States is how to use some of the Arctic's hidden resources, such as oil, without endangering this last great wilderness and its wildlife. A second, related problem is what to do about the welfare of native people in the Arctic. Their lives have changed drastically, resulting in poverty, alcoholism, and shattered customs. In addition, loose game laws and the use of high power rifles, snowmobiles, and motor boats have meant the slaughter of too many animals.

Concerns about wildlife and wild places have not been ignored. Both the American and Canadian governments have set aside huge tracts of Arctic lands as preserves. No one, least of all governments, can assume any more that North America's magnificent tundra will always be there just because it always has been. Its future now lies in human hands.

GLOSSARY

adaptation   a characteristic of function, form, or behavior that improves an organism's survival chances in a particular habitat

archipelago   a related group of islands

carnivore   meat-eating animal

circumpolar   surrounding one of the poles; the range of an animal if it follows a high latitude around the globe

colony   a group of animals nesting or breeding in a fairly confined area

conifer   a plant that bears seeds in cones, especially needle-leaved trees

consumer   an animal, so named because it must eat, or consume, to live

cyclical   following a natural series of events that occur regularly

decomposer   an organism, most often bacteria and fungi, that consumes dead tissue and reduces it to small particles

ecosystem   a system of exchanges of food and energy between plants and animals and their environment

environment   the total surroundings in which a plant or animal lives, including soil, water, air, and organisms

esker   a long, narrow ridge or mound of gravel, sand, and rocks deposited by a glacier

glacier   a massive river of ice that forms on high ground when snowfall exceeds summer melting

habitat   an animal's or plant's immediate surrounding; its specific place within the community

herbivore   plant-eating animal

invertebrate   an animal without a backbone

migrate   to make a predictable and seasonal movement from one location to another some distance away

niche   an organism's role or job in the community

omnivorous   the capability to eat both plant and animal material

permafrost   permanently frozen soil

pingo   a low hill or mound forced upward by frost action in a permafrost zone

polygon   a geometric pattern in the ground resulting from frost upheaval

predator   an animal which kills and feeds on other animals

producer   a green plant, so named for its ability to manufacture, or produce, food

prolific   capable of producing an abundance of offspring

relict   an area left unchanged after similar areas around it have been altered or destroyed

species   a group of plants or animals whose members reproduce naturally only with other plants or animals of the same group; a particular kind of plant or animal, such as a snow goose or Arctic hare

taiga   northern coniferous forest, especially in the transition zone between tundra and forest

transpiration   the process by which water evaporates from plant tissues

tree line   the level—altitude or latitude—at which trees can no longer grow

tussock   a tuft or raised clump of grass or sedge in a wet area

TUNDRA SITES

The following is a sampling of outstanding sites where you can expect to find characteristic plants and animals of the tundra and outstanding tundra scenery:

CANADA

Manitoba
Churchill, Manitoba, and the surrounding area
Northwest Territories
Auyuittuq National Park, Pangnirtung, Northwest Territories
McConnell River Migratory Bird Sanctuary, Eskimo Point
Yukon Territory
Kluane National Park, west of Whitehorse, Yukon

UNITED STATES

Alaska
Aluetian Islands National Wildlife Refuge, Cold Bay, Alaska
Arctic National Wildlife Range, Fairbanks, Alaska
Clarence Rhode National Wildlife Refuge, Bethel, Alaska
Denali National Park, McKinley Park, Alaska
Gates of the Arctic National Park, Bettles, Alaska
Katmai National Monument, King Salmon, Alaska
Kodiak Island National Wildlife Refuge, Kodiak, Alaska
Colorado
Rocky Mountain National Park, Estes Park, Colorado (alpine tundra)
New Hampshire
Presidential Range, White Mountains National Forest, Laconia, New Hampshire
(alpine tundra)

ACTIVITIES

Here are some activities and projects that will help you learn more about the Arctic tundra:

1. Find out the measurements—shoulder height, length, girth (distance around the middle)—of a grizzly bear. Put chairs, boxes, desks or other handy objects together in the approximate form of a bear to show the animal's great size.

2. To complement your study of the Arctic tundra, read about the life of the Arctic seas and report on the relationship of plants and animals in that environment.

3. Research the native people of the Arctic. Explain how they were able to live in the Far North for centuries without modern conveniences. Tell how life has changed for native people in the Arctic.

4. Write an essay defending the value of Arctic wilderness that most people will never see.

5. Create a collage of Arctic plants and animals.

INDEX

Numbers in boldface type refer to photo pages.